Israel: the theocratic state

For my Mother Helen and Nana Carol,
for always being there during my short seventeen and a half
years of life so far. Also to my mother for proof reading this
book even though you had no idea what it was about.

Israel: the theocratic state

David Hall

Published by David Hall

2014

Contents

Author's note	I
Prologue	II
Brief history of Israel	1
Religious organisation	4
Political control	6
Control of the media	11
Control of education	16
Control of the military	18
Religious reasons for founding	21
Opposition	26
Conclusion	30
Bibliography	31

Author's note

Dear reader,

Thankyou for purchasing this book, I hope you enjoy reading it.
The idea for this book started firstly in an AS level history lesson whilst learning about John Calvin's Geneva being a theocratic state. It was mentioned that Israel is a theocracy as a modern day comparison. Upon searching for a book about it, nothing came up. Therefore, I decided to write one. It is an honour to produce the first book on this topic area and to start the historical debate.

Prologue

A theocratic state is a state which is considered to be ruled by a god or many gods. It can also be ruled by an organisation or individual who are convinced that the god or gods have chosen them to be their authority and voice on earth. An example of this is the Pope as the Catholic ruler on earth, chosen by God during the conclave period. The Pope's state is Vatican City in Rome, Italy.

Furthermore, a theocratic state has rules made and enforced according to the ruling religion's beliefs. Going back to the example of the Pope, the rules in Vatican City are absolutist and Catholic, which are influenced by the teachings and commandments in the Bible.

Also, the rules in a theocratic state would penetrate all aspects of life such as: religious, military, work, education, home and social. Lastly, a theocratic state would have a repressive, authoritarian regime which would punish anyone or organisation which is suspected or found guilty of breaking or going against the rules in place.

One feature of a theocratic state is a strong religious reason or reasons for the founding of the state. This is because then the god or gods become a factor in the state's core founding principles. Another feature is a controlling religious organisation. This is because this factor gives the religion a dominating presence and the ability to implement their religious beliefs. One more feature is the religious control over politics and the state political sphere. This is because a political system heavily influenced by religion gives the theocratic regime more power. Another feature of a theocratic state is religious control over the media. This includes broadcasts and written works such as books and newspapers. This is because religious control over this factor enables the religion to indoctrinate the state's citizens with propaganda. A final feature is religious control over the state uniformed military or militia. Control over this factor allows the religion to easily suppress anyone who is against the regime and to also maintain public order exactly the way they want.

However, a state would not be considered fully theocratic if there is clear and dangerous opposition which realistically threatens to end religious control and dominance over the state.

It is my belief that, through examining the statistics and facts, Israel is a theocratic state because the evidence satisfies the requirements of the features of a theocratic state. However, although there are oppositions to Israel, it is not enough to convince me that they can bring about the end of Israel and Jewish dominance over the state.

Brief history of Israel

Israel is a small country situated in the Middle East. It is the religious birthplace of the Abrahamic religions and Hebrew language. The land of Israel is considered sacred by three of the major world religions. They are: Judaism, Christianity and Islam. Israel has come under the control of many empires, some include: Roman, Babylonian, Christian, Muslim, Ottoman and British. For this reason and also the fact of mass European immigration, Israel contains are variety of ethnicities.

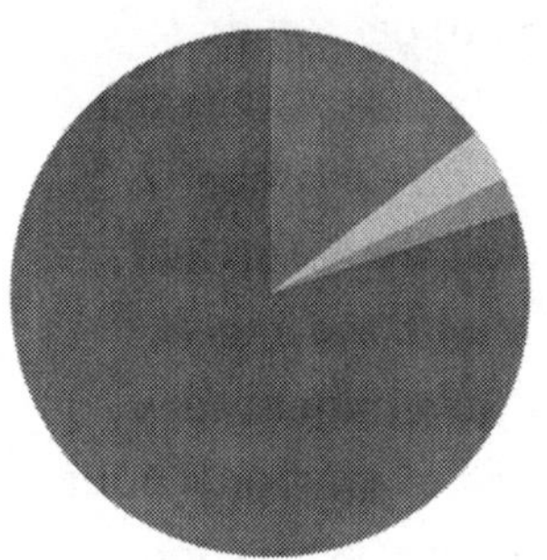

Despite this fact, Hebrew is the official language. This is because, as shown by the pie chart[1], Judaism is the dominating religion by far.

The end of the Second World War brought a fall in imperialism and overseas European colonialism. The influences of mainly Britain and France declined the most in Asia and the Middle East. Territories which were mandated after the First World War were given independence. However, Palestine, which was under a British mandate, was reformed for the creation of territory which would become a

---

[1] go.hrw.com

Jewish homeland known as Israel. This decision sparked Arab fury and also created feelings of hate and resentment towards the new state and its citizens.

The state of Israel was proclaimed on May 14, 1948 following the United Nations General Assembly on November 29, 1947 which voted in favour of Resolution 181, which was the partitioning of Palestine for Jewish and Arab sections. The Arabs called these moments al-nakba, meaning the catastrophe.

This vote followed the Balfour Declaration of 1917 which led the large Jewish communities worldwide to believe that Britain was in favour of the creation of a Jewish state in the Middle East. The Declaration was written on November 2, 1917 by Arthur James Balfour and sent to Lord Rothschild which stated that Britain had "sympathy with the Jewish Zionist aspirations[2]" and "His Majesty's Government view with favour the establishment in Palestine of a national home for the Jewish people.[3]" However, also in the Declaration stated that "nothing shall be done which may prejudice the civil and religious rights of the existing non-Jewish communities in Palestine.[4]"

Despite this last claim in the Declaration, by 1949, Israel had captured large amounts of Palestinian territory. The only

---

[2] Balfour Declaration, 1917
[3] Ibid
[4] Ibid

remaining parts were Gaza next to Egypt and the West Bank next to Jordan.

The creation of Israel has obviously become subject to many 'international Jewry' conspiracy theories. One such theory states that the United States and the rest of the world did not willingly agree to the creation of Israel. Instead, many countries were either bribed or threatened to vote in favour of Israel. This theory also states that Israel is single-handedly responsible for the ethnic cleansing and genocide of Palestinians to create enough space for the Jews. The truthfulness of his theory is highly questionable as the Balfour Deceleration states British intentions to willingly push for the creation of Israel.

Religious organisation

A Chief Rabbi is "the chief religious minister of a national Jewish community.[5]" Therefore, the most prestigious Chief Rabbis are those of Israel. This is logical because Pope Francis I, the current Pope and world leader of Catholicism, resides in the word base for Catholicism, Italy. Going by this same trend, the highest Chief Rabbis must reside in the world base for Judaism which is Israel.

There are currently two Chief Rabbis. One is the Sephardi Chief Rabbi and the other is the Ashkenazi Chief Rabbi. This idea has been in Israel since 1922 when the British recognised the authority of two Chief Rabbis and the idea has remained ever since.

The current Ashkenazi Chief Rabbi is David Baruch Lau, born 1966 in Tel Aviv. He is a reserve soldier in the Israeli Defence Force Intelligence Corps. He holds the rank of Major. Lau is also the first Rabbi to conduct responsa, a written reply by a Rabbi on a question concerning Jewish law, over the internet. On top of this, he appears regularly on radio programmes about Jewish law. Furthermore, he has published a book titled Maskil LeDavid, 2008, which focuses on: genealogy, conversions, military law and other matters.

The current Sephardi Chief Rabbi is Yitzhak Yosef, born 1952. He is the author of a very popular set of Jewish books which

---

[5] www.thefreedictionary.com

focuses on Jewish law. His books are called Yalkut Yosef. He is both a Rabbi and judge.

The religious organisation and positions of Chief Rabbi show that Israel is a theocratic state because they penetrate many aspects of life and heavy influence many aspects of Israel. Thy both penetrate the religious side of life in Israel as they have works concerning Jewish law in practice. This also influences: the media, military and education in Israel because their published books and appearances on the radio and internet would be broadcast to every Israeli and taught about in schools. Furthermore, the Ashkenazi Chief Rabi influences the military through his high rank and position in the Intelligence Corps of the Israeli Defence Force and the Sephardi Chief Rabbi influences Israel's legal system through his position as a judge. This gives the country, Israel, a very controlling religious organisation.

Political control

Israel's political sphere is dominated by Zionist and Jewish political parties. However there are anti-Zionist and anti-Jewish parties, they never gain a significant number of votes to endanger any of the main political parties of Israel. There are six main parties in Israel.

The first party is Kadima which means forward in English. This party is centre-Zionist and firmly believes that Israel is a democratic Jewish state and the national home of the Jewish people. Kadima is in support of a capitalist economy.

The second party is Likud which means consolidation in English. This party is conservative-Zionist and also nationalist. The party fully supports the settlement of Israeli citizens in the West Bank and Gaza. This is because Likud believes that these two territories belong to Israel. This party also supports a capitalist economy.

The third party is Avoda which is Israel's Labour Party. They are social-liberal-Zionist. This party supports peace negotiations with Palestinians and aims to remove Israeli settlements in Gaza and the West Bank. However, they do not support the giving back of Palestinian territory. Avoda is in favour of a more socialist economy.

The fourth party is Shinui which means change in English. It is liberal-Zionist and supports the West Bank Fence and the enclosure of Palestinians within the barrier. Shinui supports a socialist economy with the government privatization of public assets along with the lowering of taxes.

The fifth is Shas which is the Sephardi Religious Party. For this reason, the party is Ultra-Orthodox Jewish but has a varied approach to the issue of Palestine. This sometimes leaves the party divided in opinion. Shas supports a socialist economy.

The sixth is Mafdal which is the National Religious Party that represents all denominations of Judaism, unlike Shas which is Sephardi only. This party is religious-Zionist and believes that Israel is a Jewish state and should conform to a strict religious way of life. Mafdal opposes any form of Palestinian state and wishes to annex Gaza and the West Bank into Israel. This party also supports a socialist economy.

The main political parties of Israel show that it is a theocratic state because every party holds either, or both, Jewish and Zionist views. This makes Israel a theocracy because it shows that no matter what party is elected into government, there will always be an element of religious Jewish rule to each party's manifesto and plans. Therefore, Israel cannot escape a constant Jewish rule.

Since 1996, Israel has had five Prime Ministers, one of which has held the position twice during separate periods of time in between 1996 to the present day, and one stand-in Prime Minister in place of the elected Prime Minister's absence and inability to govern Israel.

The first Prime Minister was Benjamin Netanyahu who was born in 1949 in Tel Aviv. In 1967, aged 18, he joined the Israeli Defence Force to complete his compulsory military service. He was an elite commando and was also wounded whilst in service and discharged after six years' service. He was discharged holding the rank of Captain. In 1988, he joined Likud and was elected Chairman and the party's candidate for Prime Minister in 1993. In 1996, he finally won the elections and became Prime Minister of Israel. He served in this position for three years until 1999. He was elected Prime Minister again, under the same party, in 2009 and is the current Prime Minister of Israel.

The next Prime Minister was Ehud Barak who was born in 1942 in Kibbutz Mishmar Hasharon. In 1959, he joined the Israeli Defence Force as both a field soldier and commander. By 1982, his distinguished service had raised him to the rank of Major General. He held many high positions during his years of service, including the position as Head of Military Intelligence. In April of 1991, he was awarded Israel's highest military rank, Lieutenant General. He later retired from military service and in 1996 was elected Chairman of Avoda, the Israeli Labour Party. On May 17, 1999, he beat Benjamin Netanyahu in the elections and became Israel's Prime Minister. He completed his term in office on March 7, 2001.

The following Prime Minister was Ariel Sharon who was born in 1928 in Kfar Malal. At the time, this was pre-state Israel under British Mandate, which made him Palestinian by nationality, but he was Jewish by religion. He was involved in

Zionism from a young age and also served in the Israeli Defence Force. His service lasted more than twenty five years. When he retired, he held the rank of Major General. He also had a law degree from the Hebrew University in Jerusalem. When he retired, he entered politics and held many political and military roles such as; the Minister for Agriculture from 1977 to 1981, the Defence Minister from 1981 to 1983, the Minister for National Infrastructure and lastly the position of Foreign Minister from 1998 to 1999.

In May of 1999, he became the leader of Likud and also became the party's Chairman in September of that same year. In February of 2001, he won the elections and was Israel's new Prime Minister. Following his election, he formed the party Kadima. However on February 4, 2006 he suffered a brain haemorrhage and went into a coma to which he would never regain consciousness. He died on January 11, 2014 and since his entrance into a coma, the Deputy Prime Minister received the position of Acting Prime Minister.

This Deputy Prime Minister was Edhu Olmert who was born on September 30, 1945 in Binyamin during the British Mandate of Palestine. He was conscripted into the Israeli Defence Force and given a medical discharge after being wounded. He also has a law degree from the Hebrew University in Jerusalem. In 1973, aged 28, he joined the Likud party. However, in November 1993, he was elected Mayor of Jerusalem and served in this position until 2003 when he then became the Deputy Prime Minster to Ariel Sharon.

Following Sharon's decision to leave Likud and make his own party, Kadima, Olmert followed him. On January 5, 2006, after Ariel Sharon's entrance into a coma, Olmert became Acting Prime Minister.

In August of that year, he began to lose valuable popularity due to a successful Hezbollah attack on Israel. He resigned as Acting Prime Minister in 2009 due to charges of corruption and was later found guilty of breaching trust and bribery. He is currently working on an appeal to a sentence of one million Sheckles and six years in prison.

The last four Prime Ministers, and the current Prime Minister, show why Israel is a theocratic state because they were all members of the Israeli Defence Force, so would have been indoctrinated into the pro-Jewish way of leading and fighting for Israel. This makes Israel a theocracy as they would all take these views which that have been indoctrinated with and govern Israel in this way as Prime Minister. This must be true as they were all members of the main Israeli political parties which have Jewish Zionist views.

Control of the media

With the creation of Israel, the national radio station was renamed Kol Yisrael which means the voice of Israel. The military radio station was named Galei Tzahal. Both stations were controlled by the government. However, in 1965, Kol Yisrael became self-governing. In 1968, Israeli television came out and only dedicated one and a half hours each night to broadcasting in Arabic.

Galei Tzahal was set up in 1950 and offers: talk shows, music and traffic reports mainly. This radio station is funded by the military but the main listeners are civilians. Unlicensed radio stations do exist in Israel and broadcast: ethnic music, religious programmes and commercial broadcasts. All of these are illegal.

In 1966, the government, to which the Prime Minister was Benjamin Netanyahu, announced its intention to privatise public broadcasting. To what extent this actually happened is unknown and it is also unclear whether or not, as current Prime Minister, he intends to do it again.

The government and media of Israel established themselves together when Israel was created. Many editors and journalists worked with the Israeli government. Some even became members of t government and integrated the systems effectively. Lots of editor and journalists worked closely with Zionist groups and organisations. Members of the Editor's Committee met regularly with the Prime Minister and Defence Minister to discuss certain material which was prohibited from being published. Military mistakes and cases of corruption were brushed over and not reported.

An example of this would be the case of Moshe Dayon. He served as Israel's Army Commander during the 1956 war and later as Defence Minister in the 1967 war. He used his military position to illegally claim archaeological finds and also different transportation vehicles. None of this was reported on or published at the time.

This shows that Israel is a theocratic state because the Zionist government, ruling with Judaism, could control publishing, broadcasting and use censorship to eliminate any material which went against their beliefs. This control shows a theocracy because it religiously indoctrinates viewers with selected Jewish material and also suppresses and removes any negative material which would harm the regime and encourage free thought and anti-Judaism.

Israel is said to be the most media obsessed country in the world. Situations which would be ignored in other countries end up as front page stories, simply because they happen in Israel. Israeli citizens consume the most media. They obsess heavily over media such as; watching the news, listening to the radio and reading papers. Statistically, 70% of the population of Israel are frequent internet users[6], which puts

---

[6] www.internetworldstats.com

into perspective their obsession over internet media and usage of the internet alone.

The obsession over the media can be explained by the constant state of threat Israel is under. Also, Israel is a small country so would have well connected local communities who would listen out on the radio and television for updates on military activity and deaths in combat.

The pie chart above[7] shows that out of one hundred Israeli; newspapers, magazines, radio broadcasts and television programmes, the singular dominating language is Hebrew. Although the 'other' section has a higher percentage, it includes every other language of the world apart from Arabic and Hebrew so would be in minute sections if broken down further. The chart also shows that the least used language by the Israeli media is Arabic, which would be the main language of Palestinians.

---

[7] www.abyznewslinks.com

There are six main newspapers in Israel, all of them were featured in the list of 100 newspapers.

The first is Haaretz which is a morning newspaper, owned by the Schocken family. This is obviously a pro-Israel and Jewish newspaper. There is a tab titled 'Jewish World' on the homepage and there are lots of advertisements for learning Hebrew. There are also many advertisements and campaigns to buy products from Israel. There are only English and Hebrew language options and the articles are pro-Israel. For example, the 'breaking news' banner shuns Hamas and glorifies the Israeli Defence Force.

 The second is Yediot Aharonot which is an afternoon paper and owned by the Moses family. This newspaper is pro-Israel but less so than Haaretz because it also has a 'Jewish' section but does not have any Israeli advertisement and is available only in English. However, the articles are pro-Israel Defence Force and very critical of Hamas.

The third is Ma'ariv which is an afternoon paper and is owned by the Nimrodi family. This newspaper is the most nationalist out of the main six newspapers. The flag of Israel flies boldly and strong Israeli Defence Force soldiers are shown at the top of the newspaper. There is a 'Jewish' and also a 'Zionist' section. The top story tells people to hang a flag, of Israel, and support the military. This newspaper is only available in Hebrew so had to be translated online into English.

The fourth is the Jerusalem Post which is owned by foreign investors whose names are not available for public viewing. This paper is as much pro-Israel as Haaretz because there is a 'Jewish section' tab and there are many Jewish and Zionist advertisements. The only language options are English and French. The articles are very sympathetic towards the Israeli Defence Force and hostile towards Hamas.

The fifth is Yisrael Ha-Yom which is a free newspaper that is distributed daily and relies on advertising revenues to keep operational. This newspaper appears to be the least pro-Israel. There is a Hebrew alternative only and the articles are in favour of Israel and against Gaza and Hamas. However, there are no Jewish or Zionist sections or advertisements.

The sixth is Makor Rishan-Hasofeh which is a right-wing, nationalist newspaper. However, there is no online version of this newspaper so it is not available to anyone outside of Israel. For this reason and facts about it, it must be assumed that it is on par or more pro-Israel than Ma'ariv.

The six main newspapers of Israel make it a theocratic state because no matter how much or how little pro-Israel they are, none of them sympathise with Palestine or Gaza. This creates a negative social view towards them in Israel. These negative views are exactly what the government, which are Zionist and Jewish, want.

Control of education

The current Israeli Minister of Education is Shai Piron who was born on January 25, 1965 in Kfar Vitkin. He is a Rabbi and Private in the Israeli Defence Force. He also holds a degree in law from Shaarei Mishpat College. Shai is a member of the political party Yesh Atid.

This party means there is a future in English and was founded in 2012 by Yair Lapid, who is a Zionist. The party claims to be centralist and believes that Israel is a Jewish state whose democracy and existence has been built on the visions of the Prophets of Israel.

This information proves that Israel is a theocratic state because the Minister for Education is a Rabbi and a member of a Zionist religious party. These views of his own Jewish belief and that of the party would filter into the education system so would indoctrinate school children into believing the Jewish Zionist views.

Secondary school student who pass their mandatory examinations are awarded a Bagrut Certificate by the National Ministry for Education. The certificate, if a pass at a good level, can lead to acceptance into: jobs higher education and elite military units.

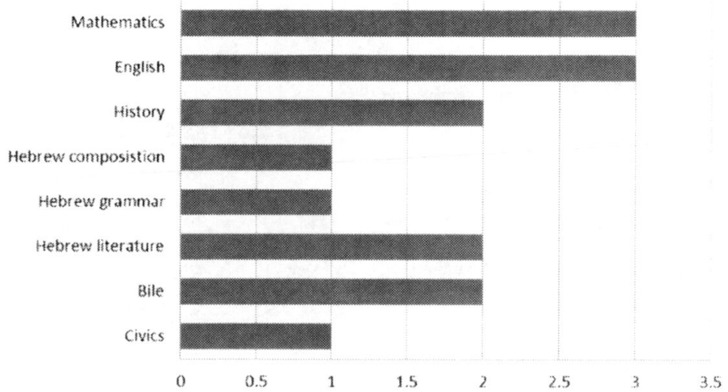

The bar graph above[8], where the Y axis is the required subject of study and the X axis is the minimum level of study needed, shows that most of the required studies are related to Judaism. For example; civics would be the study of Jewish law and the study of Israeli society, Bible would be the study of the Torah, the Hebrew subjects would be linguistic studies and history would be ancient Biblical Jewish and modern day Jewish history.

The education system in Israel shows that it is a theocratic state because the mandatory subjects needed to achieve the Bagrut Certificate are dominated by Judaism. These would be indoctrinating and would fail anyone who thought differently or went against the taught information. This makes the education system oppressive and highly in favour of the religion, Judaism.

---

[8] Fulbright.org.il

Control of the military

This image[9] shows the emblem of the Israeli Defence Force, which is the name of Israel's armed forces. As shown by the picture, a morphed form of the Star of David features prominently in the centre of the logo.

This shows that Israel is a theocratic state because the emblem shows that Judaism has a very close relation with the military, so much so that the symbol for Judaism is on the emblem of the armed forces. Furthermore, this implies that the Israeli Defence Force is a religious military, which is there to defend the faith. If this is true, Israel is a theocracy because the main purpose of the military would be to protect and fight for Judaism.

The Israeli Defence Force claims its mission is to defend the existence of Israel and its sovereignty. However, Israel does not have a monarchy to defend so it must be assumed that by sovereignty, it is meant either the Jewish God or King David, who is the Biblical King of the Jewish people on earth. This strengthens the claim that the Israeli Defence Force is a religious military which is there to defend Judaism.

---

[9] En.m.wikipedia.org

Furthermore, like every military service man or woman, in any military around the world, members of the Israeli Defence Force are required to fight and give their lives for their country, Israel. They must also conform to five main values. These are; keeping military tradition, obeying the democratic principles and law of Israel, uphold Jewish traditions, love their homeland and keep to the universal moral codes of ethical conduct such as the sanctity of life.

These principles of the Israeli Defence Force show that Israel is a theocratic state because loving their homeland is indoctrinating soldiers into loving their homeland's religion, Judaism. Also, solders must uphold Jewish traditions which make the military orientated around religion. These two points make Israel a theocracy because it allows the leaders of the country, who are Jewish, to make easier use of the military to fight for the state religion.

The current Israeli Minister of Defence is Moshe Ya'alon, born June 24, 1950 in the Haifa suburb of Kiryat Haim in Israel. He also has a degree in political science from the University of Haifa which he received in February, 1990. Earlier in his life, he was a member of the Labour Zionist Movement. Following this at age 18, Ya'alon was drafted into the Israeli Defence Force in 1968 and retired on June 1, 2005 holding the rank of Lieutenant General.

He joined Likud in 2008 and the next year he became Vice Prime Minister and Minister of Strategic Affairs. In March

2013, whilst continuing to hold these two positions, he also became Israel's Minister of Defence.

The current Israeli Chief of General Staff is Benjamin Gantz who was born June 9, 1958 in Kfar Ahim. In 1977, aged 18, he was conscripted into the Israeli Defence Force. He also holds many academic degrees such as history from Tel Aviv University and political science from the University of Haifa. On February 13, 2011 he became Chief of General Staff and was promoted to Lieutenant General.

These two people show that Israel's military constitutes it being a theocracy because the Defence Minister would have strong Zionist and Jewish views, due to his political affiliation, so would move in favour of military action which would benefit Judaism. Also, the Chief of General Staff must have these views as he would take his orders from the Minister of Defence and Prime Minister, who are both members of Likud and are Zionists.

Religious reasons for founding

If Israel has been founded and exists on religion, then it is a theocratic state because religion, in this case Judaism, and God are at the centre of Israel's foundations. For this claim to be true, three statements must be proven true through scripture.

Firstly, the Jewish people must be God's chosen people as this proves they have a relationship, with God, like no other person could.
Secondly, the land of Israel must be the chosen land for the chosen people because if it is not, Jewish people do not have a claim to possess it.
Thirdly, the chosen land, being Israel if the previous statement is true, must be promised to the Jewish people by God because then they have a full claim to own the land.

The Jewish people are clearly shown to be God's chosen people in Deuteronomy because it says "thou art an holy people unto the Lord thy God: the Lord thy God hath chosen these to be a special people unto himself, above all people that are upon the face of the earth.[10]" this passage states that God has picked out the Jewish people, because he loved them, to be his special people who are greater than any other religion or race.

---

[10] Deuteronomy 7:6-8

This claim is backed up in Isaiah when God says to Isaiah, who is Jewish, "ye are my witness, saith the Lord, and my servant who I have chosen[11]" because "he hath glorified thee.[12]" This shows again that God has specifically chosen the Jewish people as the most special of all the people and even gives them recognition by glorifying them.

Also, in Ezekiel, God says "ye [the Jews] shall be my people, and I will be your God.[13]" This use of personal pronouns strengthens the argument that the Jewish people alone are Gods chosen people. Therefore, through scripture, the claim that the Jews are God's chosen people is true.

The land of Israel is also shown to be the chosen land for the chosen people. Psalms states that "the earth is the Lord's, and the fullness thereof; the world, and they that dwell therein.[14]" This means that God is in charge of all the land on earth and all the inhabitants. This means that only he has the power to allocate land.

In Genesis, Israel is specifically allocated to the Jewish people because it says "and the Lord appeared unto Abraham, and said, unto thy seed will I give this land: and there builded he an altar unto the Lord, who appeared unto him.[15]" The land

---

[11] Isaiah 43:10
[12] Isaiah 60:9
[13] Ezekiel 36:28
[14] Psalms 24:1
[15] Genesis 12:7

that God told Abraham he would give him and the generations after him is Israel.

This giving of the land is also stated in Deuteronomy because it says "behold, I have set the land before you: go in and possess the land which the Lord sware unto your fathers, Abraham, Isaac, and Jacob, to give unto them and to their seed after them.[16]" This is further told to the Jewish people through Ezekiel because God says "and ye shall dwell in the land that I gave to your fathers.[17]" This land which was given to the fathers is stated previously in Genesis as being Israel.

Even though the specific name Israel is not mentioned, it is told geographically in Numbers when God commands Moses to "speak unto the Children of Israel, and say unto them, when ye are passed over Jordan into the land of Canaan; then ye shall drive out all the inhabitants of the land from before you...and dwell therein: for I have you the land to possess it.[18]" This proves that the land God set aside for the Jewish people is Israel because the modern day boarders are almost the same as the land of Canaan mentioned in the Bible.

Israel is also said in Genesis and Joshua because in these books, God says to the Jews "for all the land which thou seest, to thee I will give it, and to thy seed for ever.[19]" Also,

---

[16] Deuteronomy 1:8
[17] Ezekiel 36:28
[18] Numbers 33:51-53
[19] Genesis 13:15

"every place that the sole of your foot shall tread upon, that have I given unto you, as I said unto Moses.[20]" This also proves that God gave Israel to the Jewish people because after escaping slavery in Egypt, the Jews first saw and set foot on the land of Canaan which is now modern day Israel. For these reasons, through scripture, the idea that the chosen land for the chosen people is Israel is true.

The chosen land, to which has been proven to be Israel, is further shown to be promised to the Jewish people by God in Genesis because God says "and I will establish my covenant [an agreement between humans and God] between me and thee and thy seed after thee in their generations for an everlasting covenant, to be a God unto thee, and to thy seed after thee. And I will give unto thee, and thy seed after thee, the land wherein thou art a stranger, all the land of Canaan, for an everlasting possession; and I will be their God.[21]" It was established in the last point that Canaan is modern day Israel. The covenant here shows God agreeing, promising, to give Israel to the Jewish people and all the generations after them from Ancient Biblical times to the present day and forever more.

Also, it is said in Psalms that "he hath remembered his covenant forever, the word which he commanded to a thousand generations. Which covenant he made with Abraham, and his oath unto Isaac; and confirmed the same

------

[20] Joshua 1:3
[21] Genesis 17:7-8

unto Jacob for a law, and to Israel for an everlasting covenant: saying, unto thee will I give the land of Canaan, the lot of your inheritance.[22]" This covenant also shows the same promise to the Jewish people because it states that he will always remember his promise, covenant. This further shows that he will deliver on his agreement, which also shows his covenant is a promise.

Furthermore, God did not lie to the Jewish people because in Psalms he also says "my covenant which I will break.[23]" The mentioning of a covenant in scripture, which God will never forget or break, shows that the land of Israel has been promised to the Jewish people.

Due to the fact that through scripture, all three statements have been proven true, Israel is a theocratic state because the Jewish people have a strong, undeniable, religious claim to Israel.

---

[22] Psalms 105:8-11
[23] Psalms 89:34-36

Opposition

Despite all the claims that Israel is a theocratic state, the existence of opposition does not allow for the argument that Israel is fully a theocratic state. There are three main opposing factors that prevent Israel from being fully theocratic.

The first is the United Nations. On November 29, 2012 the United Nations accepted Palestine as a non-member observer state with only nine countries opposing the vote out of 147. This is opposition to Israel as the acceptance of Palestine undermines the Jewish claim to the land. This therefore contests, but does not negate, Israel's religious hold over Israel.

The second is a group known as Hamas. This group is a militant, fundamentalist, Islamic organisation which was founded in 1987 during the First Intifada, an uprising by Muslims against the Jewish settlers of Israel. Hamas is an acronym for the Arabic phrase Harakat Al-Muqawama Al-Islamia, which means Islamic Resistance Movement in English. They currently operate from the West Bank and Gaza and are involved in: religious, militaristic and political activities. For example, they run and control: schools, hospitals and religious institutions.

Hamas have five main beliefs and aims which are; the formation of an Islamic, authoritarian, Palestinian state, the destruction of Israel, the non-recognition of the state of

Israel, the belief that Israel is an unlawful occupying power and the belief that resistance to Israel is a religious duty.

Hamas claim not to be anti-sematic, only anti-Zionist. However, this is difficult to believe while they hold the belief that the holocaust never happened, holocaust denial.

The military division of Hamas is called Izzedine al Qassam and these military brigades were set up in the 1990's.There are around 7,000-10,000 soldiers and a potential 20,000 reservists with an annual budget of £30-41 million.

The brigades became a uniformed military organisation after Hamas took control of Gaza by ousting their rival party, Fatah, in a civil war. For this reason, Hamas' popularity is on a steep increase.

Despite the success of Hamas among the Muslim community, they are considered a terrorist organisation by the: United States of America, United Kingdom, European Union and Israel.

The existence of a group like Hamas directly comes into conflict with Israel's ambitions to annex Gaza and the West Bank. Furthermore Hamas' strong Muslim orientation comes heavily into conflict religiously with Israeli Judaism. Hamas is a dangerous problem for Israel as they share boarders and Hamas is willing to fight and die in order to remove Israel's power from what they believe to rightfully be Palestine.

The third is Orthodox Judaism. They believe that the cause of Israel is Zionism, which is wrong. Zionism is defined as "the political movement started by Austrian journalist Theodor Herzl who concluded that the only way to end Jewish suffering was to create a home in Palestine.[24]"

Orthodox Judaism opposes Zionism because they believe God will grant the Jewish people the Kingdom of Israel. However, Israel was created with armies and therefore serves only as materialistic salvation. This is a falsification of the Jewish perspective on salvation because the only route to salvation is to get closer to God. Materialism is seen as a distraction and regresses someone's potential for salvation. Orthodox Judaism therefore opposes Israel and the system because it damages people's chances of salvation.

Also, Orthodox Judaism opposes Zionism because they believe Zionists are distant from Judaism and the Torah. Orthodox Judaism would then oppose Israel because it could be seen as built upon misconceptions of true Judaism and incorrect interpretations some people have had once the idea of Zionism led them astray from the real teachings of the Torah.

Furthermore, Orthodox Judaism believes Zionism goes against God's commandment, especially Exodus 20:13 which states that you will not kill. This is believed because Zionism is fencing in Palestinians, like the West Bank Barrier, which

---

[24] www.urbandictionary.com

resembles the Nazi concentration and death camps in Europe where they were imprisoned and murdered. This is unacceptable for Orthodox Jews because they believe that Zionism misuses the Torah and Jewish lives to oppress others wrongfully and to also further their own political interests.

The existence of these three oppositions prevents Israel from being fully a theocratic state as they threaten the Jewish control over Israel. However, they do not have the necessary power to prevent Israel from being a theocracy because they are not strong enough to end the Jewish dominance and control, in the form of Zionism, over Israel.

For example; even though the United Nations did vote in favour of Palestine, some countries did oppose, Hamas is powerful and influential but they are not strong enough to successfully combat the Israeli Defence Force and the views of Orthodox Judaism are not universal. This means that not every Orthodox Jew accepts the stated views.

Conclusion

Through the examination of the evidence, it must be concluded that Israel is indeed a theocratic state. This is because Israel's government is dominated by Zionist Jewish parties, which means that Judaism heavily influences Israeli politics. This government controls the; media, education and military so these religious principles, which the government hold and rule with, would be put into place in these sections also. Furthermore, it is shown through scripture that Israel was founded on religious principles. Lastly, Israel has a very strong and dominating religious organisation and presence through Judaism's Chief Rabbis of Israel's ability to influence the government and sections that it controls.

Bibliography

Brief history of Israel

go.hrw.com/atlas/norm_htm/Israel.htm

history.howstuffworks.com/cold-war/the-cold-war-timeline1.htm

news.bbc.co.uk/1/hi/world/middle_east/7381315.stm

www.hitorytoday.com/richard-cavendish/foundation-state-israel

www.ifamericansknew.org/history/realstory.html

www.historylearningsite.co.uk/balfour_decleration_of_1917.htm

Balfour Declaration, 1917

Religious organisation

www.thefreedictionary.com/Chief+Rabbi

www.catholic.org/pope/

www.jpost.com/Opinion/Op-Ed-Contributors/Two-Chief-rabbis-is-one-too-many-338695

mfa.gov.il/MFA/AboutIsrael/State/Personalities/Pages/Ashkenazi-Chief-Rabbi-David-Lau.aspx

www.nybueprint.com/rabbi-david-baruch-lau-ashkenazic-chief-rabbi-israel

mfa.gov.il/MFA/AboutIsrael/State/Personalities/Pages/Sephardi-Chief-Rabbi-Yitzhak-Yosef.aspx

Political control

judaism.about.com/od/politics/a/potparties.htm

www.bbc.co.uk/news/world-middle-east-21073450

judaism.about.com/od/politics/a/primeministers.htm

mfa.gov.il/mfa/aboutisrael/state/pages/Benjamin%20netanyahu.aspx

www.jewishvirtuallibrary.org/jsource/biography/netanyahu.html

www.bbc.co.uk/news/world-middle-east-18008697

www.bioraphy.com/people/benjamin-netanyahu-9421908

mfa.gov.il/MFA/MFA-Archive/2001/Pages/Ehud%20Barak.aspx

www.jewishvirtuallibrary.org/jsource/biography/barak.html

mfa.gov.il/MFA/MFA-Archive/2003/Pages/Ariel%20Sharon.aspx

www.jewishvirtuallibrary.org/jsource/biography/sharon.html

www.bbc.co.uk/news/world-middle-east-11746593

www.bioraphy.com/people/ariel-sharon-9480655

www.jewishvirtuallibrary.org/jsource/biography/olmert.html

www.bioraphy.com/people/ehud-olmert-40512

Control of the media

www.abyznewslinks.com/issue.htm

www.jewishvirtuallibrary.org/jsource/isdf/text/widlanshi.ht
ml

www.internetworldstats.com/middle.htm

www.jewishvirtuallibrary.org/jsource/Society_&_Culture/ele
tronic_media.html

www.haaretz.com/#wrapper [Tuesday July 29, 2014]

www.ynetnews.com/home/0,7340,L-3083,00.html [Tuesday
July 29, 2014]

translate.google.co.uk/translate?hl=en&sl=iw&u=http://ww
w.nrg.co.il/&prev=/search%3Fq%3Dmaariv%2Bnewspaper%2
6client%3Dsafari%26sa%3DX%26hl%3Den%26biw%3D1024%
26bih%D671 [Tuesday July 29, 2014]

www.jpost.com/?Mobileid=1 [Tuesday July 29, 2014]

www.jpost.com/EditionFrancaise/Home.aspx [Tuesday July 29, 2014]

www.israelhayom.com/site/today.php [Tuesday July 29, 2014]

<u>Control of education</u>

Cms.education.gov.il/educationcms/units/owl/english/aout/ministry+structure.htm

www.knesset.gov.il/mk/eng/mk_eng.asp?mk_individual_id_t=886

www.jewishvirtuallibrary.or/jsource/politics/yeshatid.html

Fulbright.org.il/en/?page_id=1286

<u>Control of the military</u>

en.m.wikipedia.org/wiki/Israel_Defence_Forces#/image/File:Badge_of_the_Israel_Defence_Forces.svg

www.knesset.gov.il/mk/eng/mk_eng.asp?mk_individual_id_t=823

www.likud.org.il/en/members-of-the-knesset/moshe-bogie-ya'alon

www.jewishvirtuallibrary.org/jsource/biography/Benny-Gantz.html

www.mfa.gov.il/mfa/aboutisrael/state/personalities/pages/ennny_ganz.aspx

www.idfblog.com/about-the-idf/idf-code-of-ethics/

<u>Religious reasons for founding</u>
(all quotes have been taken from an English King James Version of the Bible)

Deuteronomy 7:6-8

Isaiah 43:10

Isaiah 60:9

Ezekiel 36:28

Psalms 24:1

Genesis 12:7

Numbers 33:51-53

Deuteronomy 1:8

Genesis 13:15

Joshua 1:3

Genesis 17:7-8

Psalms 105:8-11

Psalms 89:34-36

<u>Opposition</u>

www.un.org/News/Press/docs/2012/ga11317.doc.htm

www.blog.standforisrael.org/issues/terrorism/hamas

edition.cnn.com/2012/11/16/world/means/hamas-explainer/

www.informationclearinghouse.info/article1506.htm

www.nkusa.org/aboutus/zionsm/opposition.cfm

www.urbandictionary.com/define.php?term=zionism

CPSIA information can be obtained at www.ICGtesting.com
Printed in the USA
BVOW03s0039070115

382202BV00006B/98/P